# *Funny Things Mama Said and Did*

By Kevin D. Brady

Copyright Protected: February 21, 2017

1948-2014

# *Funny Things Mama Said and Did*

My mother, Lula Brady, passed away from a stroke on August 28, 2014.  Other than being a very beautiful woman who in her senior year of high school was crowned the 1966 Debutante Queen, she had a friendly heart and was one of the funniest people you ever wanted to meet.  She would often make us laugh with the things she would say and do.  She just had a natural way with letting funny stuff flow from her mouth like none other.  For example, she once told me upon finding out that I had started smoking cigarettes at age 30 to either stop or to take out a hundred thousand dollar life insurance policy

and make her the beneficiary.  Her logic was that if I were foolish enough to start smoking which was something she never did, at least she could get rich because of it.  She was like an undiscovered comedienne who simply never got discovered.
Since I lost her two and a half years ago, I often sit and reflect on different things she said and did and find myself either laughing to myself or starting to feel teardrops form in my eyes.  I chose to write about some of those things in order to help lighten up other people's days a little and give them a chance to meet my mom, Lula, the Undiscovered Comic, and let them get to know her as I did.

## Early Humor

In the late 1950's when my mom was a preteen she used to go out with her mother, my grandmother, to different wealthy white people's houses to clean them in the Ft. Lauderdale/Coral Gables, Florida area.  My grandma would go to a different house each day of the week and reserve that particular day for that particular person's home for as long as she could manage.  These white folks had exquisite mansions with yachts docked in the rear quite often and were meticulous about their house cleaning not wanting to even see one single pubic hair left in the bathroom sink or tub. She told us that some would put a white glove on and check behind my grandma for dust she had left behind.  Mama experienced discrimination firsthand by being told to use separate bathrooms other than the main bathroom when she and my grandma housecleaned; although it did not work with mama since she always managed to slip and use the main one.  My grandma would scold her about it if she caught her, and sometimes the boss lady would find out by getting a whiff of the scent still in the restroom and would chastise my grandma about it.  Mama told us that she felt that if she had to clean a restroom, she could have the honor of using it too.  She told us these stories later in life and told us that felt sure that if she had come along in slavery times she knew for a fact that she would have been hanged for disobedience and for talking back.

One day, one of these rich boss ladies asked my mom to follow her since she had a little something that she thought mama could do to help my grandma out with the house cleaning.  She took my mom who was a pre-teen at the time to the huge kitchen and asked her if she could clean the floor.  Mama said that she asked her where her mop was.  The woman told her that she didn't believe in mops and didn't own one.  She even told her that my grandma always cleaned it by getting on her knees with a brush, rag, and a pale.  My mom said that she told her, "I guess it won't get cleaned then!"  That's when the woman reportedly let out a sigh of disgust and told her with a frown that she was nothing like her mother and then went and told my grandma about it.  Grandma scolded her about it, but gave her something else to do instead.  Mom says that sometime later, the lady and her husband took a liking to her for her boldness and spunk and started letting her fish with them in their lake out of my grandma's way whenever they came to clean their house.


**The Muslim**


    One day in the early 70's when I was a toddler, a Muslim guy was reportedly walking through our Ft. Lauderdale, FL, neighborhood and was stopping by people's houses with literature to convert them to

Islam.  Once he knocked on our duplex apartment door, my mom cracked the door to see what he wanted.  He introduced himself and told her he was Muslim and got to informing her about how the pig was filthy and unclean to eat.  He showed her a picture of a pig with a bunch of pins sticking in it looking all nasty and told her that a pig was nothing more than a big rat.  He sniffed the scent coming from the crack in the doorway of our apartment and smelt pork cooking.  He asked her, "Is that pork cooking?"  She said, "It shole is!  A big pot of pig ears!"  He then said, "Arghhhh!" (in disgust) while shaking his head.  Then he said, "You need to throw that out!  Don't eat it!"  Mama snapped, "Man, you must be crazy as hell!  You think I'm gon throw out my dinner because YOU said to?"  He asked, "You mean you're still going to eat that?"  She said, "I shole am!  So, BYE!  I got to get back to the kitchen to my pot!"  She reportedly closed the door on him and locked it and went strutting back to the kitchen with a smile to her pot of pig ears to get a pot of rice started to cooking as well.

## Old Fashioned Butt Whoopin'

On one occasion and I assure you that it only took just ONE occasion, I as a young boy of about six years got some nerve from somewhere to bow up at my mom.  She sent word to me by my baby brother for me to come and do something, but I sent him back and told him to tell her, "I ain't gon do it!" You can imagine that he was pleased to run back and tell her something like THIS since he felt something would go down big time.  So, after he did run and tell her what I said, she stopped what she was doing and came straight to me saying, "Oh, so you ain't go do it, huh?!"  Then she wore my ass out with a switch that she kept in a corner for doing her butt whoopins.  Needless to say, I learned that she was not to be toyed with and that she meant business when she said to do something.

# The Hot Sauce

One evening, my dad came home after having some drinks with his coon hunting buddies and sat down to eat the dinner my mom had fixed.  He sat down and looked at the gravy mama had on his plate, and since it was really liquidy he referred to it as "poor man gravy".  Mama got mad and told him, "Well, a poor man is eating it ain'ta?!"  So, then, daddy proceeded to eat but began talking about how good his ex could cook.  And to make matters worse, my grandmother (his mother) who we were living with at the time added her two cents in by saying, "You know, she WAS a good cook!"  And daddy added, "Now, one thing she could do is cook."  Mama became furious and snapped, "Then why don't you go back and get that bitch!"  She never had any hard feelings for daddy's ex since she was in Florida and his ex was out in California, yet daddy pushed her button by bragging on her cooking like it was superior to hers.  So, she exploded like any other woman would have in the same circumstances.  Well, daddy proceeded to ask her for the hot sauce, and mama briskly brought it over and slammed the bottle on the table so hard that it shattered wasting all of the hot sauce out of it into a pool on the table.  A brawl then ensued which was the only time I ever seen my parents fight.  When my dad jumped on top of mama choking her on the living room floor, I, around ten at the time jumped on his back punching his head with all my might to make him let her go.  She broke away and left the house crying with me and my baby brother trailing her.  This incident almost broke them up, but daddy came to his senses and apologized to her the next day at her friend's house down the road, and all three of us returned home.  Everything returned back to normal, and my knee-baby sister was the result.

## The Water Guns

Like all other kids, my siblings and I liked water guns.  We even made us some homemade shotguns that would shoot rocks with amazing accuracy out of broomsticks, rubber bands, and clothes pins.  Mama didn't particularly like buying any type of toy guns for kids, but she surrendered and bought us all our own water guns once.  Each of us had a different color water gun.  We were so proud to have them and ran around in the yard shooting water at one another and even shot water through the window screen from the inside to the outside or vice versa.  Time has faded the exact reason for mom doing it, but one day mama got so mad at us about the water guns that she grabbed all three of them and threw them on top of our roof so that we couldn't reach them.  And that, my friends, was the end of THAT!

# Crazy Lady Next Door

During the time my knee baby sister was just learning to crawl, we lived with one of my aunts for a brief time.  Next door to my aunt's apartment lived an old woman who loved to play with her when she seen her.   She'd tickle her and make faces at her just to see her laugh and crawl really fast across the floor.  One evening the old woman came to our front screen door and scratched at the screen repeatedly while making scary noises provoking my knee baby sister to laugh hysterically and crawl across the floor with her Pamper making a tune as she did so.  After twenty minutes went by and my knee baby sister had wandered into another room of the apartment, the old woman was still standing at the door scratching at the screen as we were trying to watch T.V.  Mama looked around at us and said in a really low voice, "I don't know WHAT I'm gon have to do about this crazy ass woman!"  We burst out laughing until tears flowed from our eyes gazing at the woman who didn't know what we were laughing at so hard.  She soon left the door after she got tired of standing there.


## Lil' Girlie

There was a woman a friend of my dad met who used to love to sit and talk with my mom while her boyfriend would be outside laughing and talking with my dad about their coon hunting hobby.  My dad kept a whole team of around ten hound dogs that he would coon hunt with on various nights with his friends who loved to do the same thing.  One day this woman friend showed mama a knife and told her that this knife was her little secret in case the guy started "trippin" and she needed to protect herself.  She even gave it a name: "Lil' Girlie".  Well, one day she rode to the house with this guy and had shades on when she came in the house.  Mama seen she had black eyes once she took the shades off and started questioning her.  She told her that she and the guy had gotten into a fight.  Mama then asked, "Well, where was "Lil Girlie"?  She said that she couldn't get to her purse.  She got him back some time later though by burning his toes with a cigarette lighter while he was drunk, and even told us to go peep at his toes outside where he was with my dad if we didn't believe her.  This guy was so dark that you could barely see any difference on his toes if they WERE burned, but the woman sounded convincing that she had done what she claimed.


**The Cheese**


Mama used to get WIC for my two younger sisters when they were babies and could get milk, cheese, bread, cereal, and juice with the vouchers. But the rules were strict on exactly what you could buy, and it took a lot of trial and error on getting exactly the right size this and that.    Well, one day she walked into the old Big Star Grocery Store to buy some things with the WIC vouchers, and trouble erupted.  Everything she had picked up was right except for the cheese.  So, the cashier told her to change it to a certain ounce size, and mama went and changed it.  When she came back, the cashier told her once more that the cheese was still the wrong size.  Mama let out a loud sigh and walked to the cheese aisle for the third time.  She grabbed one after a little study and came back.  The cashier told her AGAIN that the cheese was still the wrong size. Mama grabbed the cheese and left the checkout counter mad as hell marching back to the dairy aisle. She leaned back as if she was a baseball pitcher and threw the cheese from the front of the store through the air, and it flew down the aisle and hit the floor spinning and slid to the opposite end of the aisle striking the metal casing on the bottom of the meat rack in the meat department.  Mama then stormed out of the store hollering "Damn yall AND that cheese!"  I and my other brother were rolling with laughter at the gall of our mother on doing such an act.

## Older Customer's Looks

My family operated a car wash in Statesboro, Georgia, from 1983 until 1998 at various locations around town.  Through this business, we got to know a huge range of people from the prominent, Who's Who, white collar citizens who pretty much ran the city to the everyday, average Joe citizens who helped make the wheels turn in the Statesboro community by holding down industrial jobs, farming jobs, fast food jobs, businessmen and women, etc. etc. We took pride in detailing all of our customers' vehicles regardless of their rank on the social ladder.

One senior citizen customer of ours was an older white woman whom my daddy had worked with at the ITT Grinnell plant twenty years earlier.  Daddy started showing signs of Alzheimer's Disease early on, however we failed to notice it since it was so gradual, and this made him tell  us every time this certain woman came to get her car washed how beautiful she was twenty years ago when he worked with her at the plant.  Of course, the woman would blush and be flattered by the comment, but my mom would just smile and look up to the sky like saying, "Here we go again."  Mama was not threatened by daddy's comment any way whatsoever since the woman was a senior citizen, and mama was way younger and confident in her looks.

Finally, one day the woman came up, and my dad said it again like he had several times before on each prior time the woman had gotten her car washed, "Hey, Lu!  (He called my mom Lu for short.)  See this woman right here?  Now, this was ONE beautiful woman twenty years ago!"  Then came the woman's blushing as the pattern was.  But mama decided to stop the broken record from playing over and over like it had for several car washes prior.  She said, "Waaaaaaaaaaaaaaaiiiiiiiittttttttt a minute.  Wait just ONE minute.  Now, Brady, every time this woman comes here you be like, "Hey Lu, do you know that this was ONE beautiful woman twenty years ago?  So, what are you tryin' to tell her?  That she's ugly as hell RIGHT NOW?"  This comment made us all burst out laughing as well as the woman since she was glad that mama had come to her rescue and vindicated her "present" looks once and for all.

## Correcting One of my Aunties

One day one of my aunties was holding my baby sister and telling my mom how beautiful she was. She ooohed and aaawed and rocked my sister in her arms while smiling down at her.  She then told my mom, "Lula, looks like she was cropped out of something."  Mama said, "Oh yeah."  My aunt said, "Yeah, I can't place it, but looks like she was cropped out of something she's so pretty."  Mama then responded, "Huh!  She was cropped out of something, alright!  Cropped out of MY ASS!"  My aunt laughed, but mama didn't.  Mama wasn't one to hold her tongue one bit!   Mama later told us that this aunt was trying to praise my sister's looks without giving her, the mother, credit for this prettiness.  So she said she had to put it to her like that to get her point across since they were trying to overlook HER.


**Faking Sleep**


  One night I was looking for something in the living room.  It's been over twenty years ago so I can't recall what exactly I was searching for.  But I walked past mama laying on the couch asleep and snoring.  I looked right at her face and kept on about my business of hunting for the item I was in pursuit of.  After a failed attempt on that side of the living room, I made an about face and began stepping the opposite way.  That's when my eyes met my mama's eyes as she was still lying on the sofa making snoring sounds.  This spooked the hell out of me, and I got goosebumps!  She was pretending to be sleep making snoring noises as long as my back was turned yet had her eyes wide open spying on me!

## Hiding from a Bill Collector

One day during our car detailing years at our car wash, Brady's Auto Clean-Up, my mother and I trailed behind my dad to pick him up from delivery of a vehicle that we had cleaned.  My dad was taking an excessively long time talking to the guy who owned the place about the car we had cleaned, so my mom and I were forced to sit and wait in our car beside the street in downtown Statesboro.  We just talked about this and that to kill time.  My mom cut our conversation short by telling me to duck since she spotted our insurance man driving down the street in our direction.   Since he would come to our car wash every month to get a payment on a life insurance premium they carried, he figured he'd just catch us in the streets on this particular day and save a trip. I followed suit with mama's request and ducked. After five seconds or so we peeped up and seen his car sitting at the intersection of Cherry and North Main Street waiting to turn. So, we resumed our conversation counting him to be gone. About five minutes later as we talked, we heard a horn blow. We both looked to the left, and it was him: the insurance man. He had spotted us and detoured back. He gave us his signature line; "Got anything for me today, Miss Lu?" with a grin on his face. We burst out laughing on the idea that we had been busted, and he laughed too. Apparently, he had seen us when we ducked and made it his business to come right back.

## Puttin' a Child in his Place

One of my younger brother's white friends started coming to the house once he found out where he stayed.  He loved to hear my brother laugh at things he would say.  I guess, he was something like a class clown or something.  Well, he got the notion to start teasing mama with stuff like "You got dinner ready yet?"  Mama would just laugh at his boldness and go on about her business.  The old saying that if you play with a puppy, he'll lick your mouth is absolutely true since this guy went a little too far one day.  On one particular day he decided to leave my brother and I in our living room and headed to the kitchen where mama was.  Then he said, "Woman, you got me something to eat ready back here?" That's when mama let him have it.  I heard her voice blast him from where I was standing in the living room as she told him, "Look!  I think you better take yo white ass back in that living room with yo friends and leave me the hell alone if you know what's good for you!  U got me?"  Needless to say, the guy got to stepping back to the living room.  Oddly enough, that ended his visits to our house.


## Telling Off Her Mom-in-Law


One day my mom dropped my knee-baby sister off to catch the school bus like she did every weekday morning.  I don't recall exactly why she would take her to my grandma's trailer in the mornings to catch the bus, but I guess it was so she could ride with her friends on THIS particular bus.  Well, one morning my mom was headed out the door after putting my sister on the bus and talking with my grandma for a few minutes.  She said that she felt a funny aura inside the house like grandma was giving her the cold shoulder or something and claimed that her conscience told her to stand by the door once she got outside instead of walking on to her car.  After a few moments,  she began hearing my grandma and her boyfriend talking and saying bad things about my dad and the goats that he had over at her place in a wire pin out back.  She stood by the door getting an earful, and her anger began to build.  My grandma's younger sister lived about one hundred feet away in a neighboring trailer, and she seen my mom standing by the door.  It tickled her to see my mom resorting to such tactics.  My mom burst back inside scaring the living shit out of them since they thought she was long gone.  She told them off and told my grandma it didn't make sense for her to be talking about her own son that way.  She says grandma's boyfriend froze with his spoon midair since he was eating a plate of grits at the table.  My grandma froze in her tracks too, and no one said one word while she exploded with her cussing and telling them off since they were in such shock.  My auntie next door could hear the loud tremors of the showdown all the way at her house.  My mom left the house cussing and slammed the door.  My auntie nicknamed her "hell raiser" after that.

**Shoulda Seen That Coming**

On another occasion a young man from our neighborhood was working at our carwash years later and was laughing about what had happened to another guy at one of the local clubs.  He was rolling with laughter at how some guy had punched this guy and kept saying that the guy should have been able to see it coming.  Oddly enough, the next couple days he was back at work with us and half of his face was red and swollen, and he had scars and a black eye himself.  His face looked like a monster! It was so ironic since he had just been laughing at this other guy just a few days earlier, but now the same thing had happened to HIM.  My mom approached him laughing and asked, "What the hell happened to YOU?"  The guy told her that he had gotten into a fight with a dude the previous night. Mama laughed herself to tears as she looked at him and said, "Well, looks to me like you shoulda seen THAT coming!"  After she said it, she burst out laughing so hard she made us all laugh, and the guy couldn't help but laugh his own self.


## Afterthought


I hope you enjoyed reading these things that are part of my memories of my mom!  I'm sure there are some funny things that will come to mind that mama done well after this book is printed.  They kept coming to mind even as I wrote this book forcing me to keep adding segments.

We all have good memories and bad memories of our past, but we learn to treasure the bad times as well as the good times since they help build character.  I love my mom and always will, and I will always treasure the precious moments that come to mind of the times when she was around.

# *Thank You!*

Thank you for purchasing this book!  I hope you enjoyed it!

I invite you to write a short book review on it to give me your feedback and post it on my Facebook page.

I am currently working on other books at the present time of various topics.

I look forward to having you read and enjoy them as well.

# About The Author

Kevin Brady is the eldest of five kids and a graduate of Statesboro High School (1985) and Georgia Southern University with a B.B.A. in Business Management (1998).  In 2015, he published three other books including *Ghostly Encounters*, *The Sinless House* (a book he and his wife, Charlene, teamed up on), and *A Helluva Home* .   In 2016, he published *Fat-Man: the Dream Hero* and his *K.D.Brady's Four-In-One Holiday Collection*. He has one stepson, daughter-in-law and three adorable grandkids.  He loves old car shows, ghost documentaries, reading, writing, going to church, fishing, playing lottery, and being with family and friends.  He is working on other stories that will be available as soon as they are ready.

Facebook:  https://www.facebook.com/#!/kevin.d.brady.9

Email:  kdbrady6798@yahoo.com

Book Links:

Ghostly Encounters:

https://www.createspace.com/5612057

The Sinless House:

https://www.createspace.com/5696025

A Helluva Home:

https://www.createspace.com/5824467

Fat-Man: the Dream Hero:

https://www.createspace.com/6194720

K. D. Brady's Four-In-One Holiday Collection:

https://www.createspace.com/6612177

Website:

http://kdbrady6798.wixsite.com/mysite

* 9 7 8 1 5 4 4 1 0 9 6 7 1 *